*Angels' Wings*

Previously Published Works by
*Mary Elizabeth Brantley Harvey:*

"A Southern Dream", "The Moon", "My Pet Hate",
"Of JLM, Three Year Old", "Refinery", "Deserted Derrick" in
"Ozark Moon", Fayetteville, AR
"Deserted Derrick" also in North American Book of Verse,
Vol. V, Pup Tent Poets
"Twilight" The Stars and Stripes (U.S. Army)
"Daybreak", "Let Us Sing", Brazil Gazette, Brazil, IN
"An Old Oil Town", "A Sandstorm in McCamey",
"West Texas", "Old Winter Has Had His Way",
"King Edward" McCamey News, McCamey, TX
"Poverty" The Country Bard, Madison, NJ

# Angels' Wings

*Mary Elizabeth Brantley Harvey*

Lost Creek Press
Fayetteville 2003

© 2003 by Mary Elizabeth Brantley Harvey, Author.
All rights reserved.
Manufactured in the United States of America

06   05   04   03      4   3   2   1

This book was designed by Chang-hee H. Russell / C.R.Graphics

Published by: Lost Creek Press, Fayetteville, AR 72701

No part of this book may be reproduced or transmitted in any form or by any means, electronic or mechanical, including photocopy, recording or any information storage or retrieval system, without the express written permission of the publisher, except where permitted by law.

Library of Congress Cataloging-in-Publication Data 2003-107623

Mary Elizabeth Brantley Harvey, 1920
    Angels' Wings

ISBN: 0-9664290-5-2

TO
*My husband*
*my children*
*and*
*my grandchildren*

## Contents

| | |
|---|---|
| Foreword | xiii |
| Acknowledgment | xv |
| | |
| Angels' Wings | 3 |
| An Oil Town | 4 |
| A Sandstorm in McCamey | 7 |
| West Texas | 9 |
| Old Winter Has Had His Way | 11 |
| A. M. | 12 |
| Abandoned Grave | 13 |
| ABC | 14 |
| A Southern Dream | 17 |
| A Townhouse in Maryland | 19 |
| Baby's Lament | 21 |
| Bug on a Windshield | 23 |
| Bonding | 24 |
| Beauty | 27 |
| The Closed Curtain | 29 |
| To Debbi | 30 |
| Child of Mary | 31 |
| Resurrection | 33 |
| Daybreak | 34 |

| | |
|---|---|
| Davi 1993 | 35 |
| In Memory of David M. Higgins, Jr. | 37 |
| The Moon | 38 |
| Deserted Derrick | 39 |
| Drouth | 41 |
| Escape | 42 |
| Death | 43 |
| Early Morning in a Valley | 44 |
| To My Chicks on a Rainy Day | 45 |
| Ebon on Snow | 46 |
| Emblem | 49 |
| Firefly | 50 |
| Four Years Old | 51 |
| Helda, the Stripdown | 53 |
| Highway | 55 |
| Gatsby (nicknamed Goofy) | 57 |
| King Edward | 59 |
| Interlude | 60 |
| Life | 63 |
| Last Resort | 67 |
| La Vista | 68 |
| Lost | 70 |

| | |
|---|---|
| The Bindweed | 71 |
| Mary, Age 2 | 73 |
| My Pet Hate | 74 |
| Mother | 75 |
| Mother's Death | 76 |
| Of JLM, Three-Year-Old | 79 |
| And Now We Know | 80 |
| Moving the Sheep | 81 |
| Old Man at Bedtime | 83 |
| My Uncle's Death | 84 |
| One Day in October | 85 |
| No Return | 86 |
| O.P.O. at the Vet's | 89 |
| Poverty | 90 |
| Refinery | 91 |
| Quiet Hummer | 92 |
| Power of the Pecos | 93 |
| The Dry Devil's River | 95 |
| Saturday Night | 97 |
| Soft Wind | 98 |
| See-Saw | 99 |
| Spring Sonnet | 101 |

| | |
|---|---|
| Six O'Clock, Boomtown | 102 |
| Summer Storm | 103 |
| The Boy and the Fish | 104 |
| The Balloons | 105 |
| Bears | 107 |
| Touching | 109 |
| Twilight | 110 |
| The Dive | 111 |
| U.S. Eighty West | 113 |
| Walking on Hot Coals | 115 |
| Why | 117 |
| Wet Fields | 118 |
| Woodland Trail | 119 |
| What is Age? | 121 |
| Fall | 122 |
| All Hallow's Eve | 123 |
| Yesterday | 125 |
| Your Father | 126 |
| Hats Off to Dorothy Lindquist | 127 |
| One Day | 129 |

*List of Photos and Illustrations*

| | | |
|---|---|---|
| Arkansas Building | Mary Harvey | 17 |
| Derrick in Texas | Mary Harvey | 39 |
| Helda | Mary Harvey | 53 |
| Gatsby | Mary Harvey | 57 |
| Untitled drawing | Joni Harvey Higgins | 119 |

# *Foreword*

I have always written poetry. Sometimes it was to express a girlish whimsy, the happiness of knowing the love of a good man, the joy of watching my children or hearing their voices as I went about the house; other times it was to soothe my soul in times of trouble and loss, but always it was to frame with words the emotions and the thoughts I could not speak.

In collecting these poems into one volume, I hope to leave to my children, grandchildren, and future generations a glimpse of myself, a thread by which to tie me to them and them to me with love and understanding. May they be able, even after I am gone from this life, to read my work and recognize themselves in my words and by my words know me.

**Mary E. Harvey**

# *Acknowledgment*

I acknowledge the contributions of love and support from my husband Lt. Col. Charles S. Harvey, Sr., now deceased, and my children, Charles S., Jr., Joni Higgins, also deceased, and Debbi Covey and their families. I appreciate the encouragement and help of Michael Heffernan and "Skip" Hayes and the comments of Walter Lemke from his column "Ozark Moon." Rosa Marinoni, too, generously gave me hope for my poetry.

*Angels' Wings*

# Angels' Wings

Just up the slope from Fairview's shadowed pond
where circling geese scarce roil the surface calm,
beneath a greening crabapple tree, there lies
a black granite stone engraved with name and dates
and lines from Tennyson's "In Memoriam."
Two etched angels guard with upraised wings
the likeness of the youth whose image is
forever set into the marble there.
Atop a weathered monument nearby,
a mockingbird sends out its strident melodies.
A blue jay strikes its song to scold
the killdeer bobbing down the gravel lane.

From the budding tree, a small grey wren flies down
and drops a twig upon the angels' wings.

# An Oil Town

Out in the oil fields of Texas,
Where derricks cover the land,
Live people who conquer the hardships
Of huts and wind and sand.

Shacks are the main habitations—
Shanties half-built during booms,
But the people who flock to the oil fields
Never seek for luxurious rooms.

Their money is spent when they make it
For food and liquor and cars
The men drive Buicks and Packards,
And smoke ten-cent cigars.

The picture shows do a good business,
And the night spots run at full speed,
For the people who live in an oil town
Never stay home to talk and read.

A mecca for youth are the oil fields,
For boys who want money for school.

They go to get funds for college,
But they stay to work as a rule.

Oil, like gold, causes madness,
Men rush to where it is found.
They leave for the good old oil fields,
Where black gold flows from the ground.

Found in the common oil town
Are people of every kind—
Rich men as well as the workers—
The deaf, the mute, and the blind.

Overnight there springs up a city,
A den for gamblers and crooks,
But still a place of prosperity,
Though it isn't much for looks.

The streets in the oil town are crooked;
They are usually narrow and rough;
And though people ruin their fine autos,
They say the streets are good enough.

Prices are high on the price tag,
And bargains are almost unknown.
Electric lights are common,
But seldom is found a phone.

And so an oil town arises—
To flourish and live for a day,
But after the oil is all taken,
Only a few people stay.

They rush for the latest gushers
And stay there a month or so,
But then they leave by the hundreds,
And that's where the oil towns go.

# A Sandstorm in McCamey

Have you ever seen McCamey
When a sandstorm has just struck,
And the dust is sailing through the air,
With the wind that's run amuck?

When the few little growing things are tossed
Like a willow in a storm,
And the wind howls round the houses
Wailing its weird alarm?

When the trash is whisked up from the streets
And piled against the doors,
And through each crack in the shacks so old
The raging wild wind roars?

When both the old and new floors there
Are covered by an inch or more
Of gritty sand and filmy dust
That's come through cracks in the floor?

Then you have never really seen
What our town is truly like.
You should come and stay for a little while
Till you see a sandstorm strike.

# West Texas

Long months without fresh water,
When the blistering sun beat down,
The flowers and grass all withered;
No comfort could be found.

The wind came to be dreaded;
Its breath was worse than none.
It brought more heat and terror,
And nothing could be done.

The sand filled mouths and noses,
And lingered in the air.
It meant toil for the women,
When it covered houses bare.

And then one morn when all awoke,
The sky was flecked with clouds,
And as the dinner hour drew near,
They gathered o'er like shrouds.

A pitter-patter on the roofs;
The people laughed with glee.
They filled the doors and windows,
And asked, "Oh, can it be?"

# Old Winter Has Had His Way

Stripped of all their leaves and buds,
The trees are withered and gray;
No foliage adorns them now;
Old Winter has had his way.

The little flowers that brought us joy
Long since have passed away;
Only their memory remains;
Old Winter has had his way.

The lilac that was by the walk,
Where we two met one day,
Is standing now, but wan and pale.
Old Winter has had his way.

The river is still and frozen.
Stiff are the tilting waves;
But they will dance again some time;
We've always had winter days.

# A.M.

Hurricanes striking the coast
Waves overlapping leg-waving crabs
The President dispatching our troops
to battle

Crashes on the highway
People slipping into the lake
Planes heading for distant lands

This morning
the coffee
is
strong and hot.

# *Abandoned Grave*

The stone
lies broken—
its lower half
still part of
the barren concrete base.
The ornate sculptured top
rests on the accepting earth.
Rain, wind and hail
batter the carved letters—
blind the names—
darken the dates.
Jo n Chand er Smit
came into this world
January 15, 18 1.
Departed   is earth
Octob r 9,   _
the year is gone.
The lonely grave
sinks deeper
into the mossy ground.

## ABC

A is for Andrew,
a mischievous boy
B is for baby
laughing with joy.
C is for Charlotte
who loves ballet.
D is for the doctor,
which she likes to play.
E is for elephant,
which hunters entrap.
F is for funny,
a clown with a cap.
G is for grandchildren
to sit on your lap.
H is for Heaven
where we hope to go.
I is for Indian
who shoots with a bow.
J is for jet
that flies through the air.
K is for kitten
with dark curly hair.

L is for lion
that lives in a den.
M is for Mary,
who plays violin.
N is for numbers
like seven and nine.
O is for orange,
a fruit with a rind.
P is for Peter
who makes up a rhyme.
Q is for queen
who sits on a throne.
R is for Rooster
that crows at dawn.
S is the sea
with wind and waves.
T is the tiger
that lives in a cave.
U is the umbrella
we use when rain flows.
V is for valley
where that stream goes.

W is the window
that lets in the light.
X is the X-ray
that brings bones to sight.
Y is for Yvette
with dark hair and eyes.
Z is for zebra
with stripes on his sides.
This is the end
of the ABCs
as they fade away
in the evening breeze.

# A Southern Dream

The ring of the workmen's hammers
Echoes through empty halls,
And the sound of falling plaster
Marks the end of "A Southern Dream."
The old familiar landmark stands
But a lonely shell of its former self,
And pigeons wheel about its crumbling eaves.

Parts of the massive columns have fallen
Before the onslaught of winter gales,
And the great windows have been shattered
By stones hurled by careless lads
Passing on their way from school.
Inside the big reception halls
The cherubic angels still look down,
And the beautiful winding stairway remains,
But the lingering grandeur soon will disappear
Beneath the blows of the workmen's tools,
And the Arkansas Building will be no more.

# A Townhouse in Maryland

Pine trees stretch upward
to the clouds,
their barren trunks,
bereft of needled limbs,
tower above a wooden deck
enclosed by rough board fence.
Wispy blades of grass
whisper in the wind
and flick the somber,
solitary sunflower
that shades the marigolds
and scattered toys.
Broom and rake and potted plant
stand outside the sliding door,
clover edges all
and helps the jonquil
stand erect
near curtained window.
Inside
the little tow-headed girl
watches Rug-Rat on TV

while the toddler hugs her Barney tight
and waits her turn.

Pines and clouds and blue sky
and jet trails from planes
of nearby Naval base
cover all.

# Baby's Lament

I crawled
before I walked
as most babies do—
and that was the time
when bigger brother,
bringing in the firewood,
tripped
and dropped a log
on the little finger
of my right hand.
The joint was
almost healed
and I crawled again,
but then my cousin
came to play—she
was older by
a year or so
and walking well
and running too.
Sitting on the floor
with hands palm down,
I screamed

as my cousin's foot
came down on that same
small finger joint.
At times
that bone still aches,
and it takes me back
to my crawling days.

# Bug on a Windshield

Driving along with the stereo
turned to my favorite cassette,
and listening to Guy Lombardo's band
on the windshield I heard a loud splat.

A little black blob near the side
caught my eye.
The poor small bug just flying around
met the glass of my car passing by.

There came to my mind an ad on TV
where young men on a rope
swung through the air.
Striking the wall with
stiffened feet,
they adhered to the velcro
placed there.

## Bonding

The mother drew the waking baby to her breast.
She kissed the infant as she gave a smile
and watched the nipple disappear into his mouth.
With blanket tucked around his feet to keep him warm,
she gathered two small fists into her hands.
The baby looked at her with widened eyes

reflecting back the darkness of his mother's eyes.
She felt those soft lips on her breast
and felt him reaching toward her with his hands.
She felt a tug that brought a wincing smile,
and in her palms the little feet turned warm.
The nipple slipped—a tremble crossed the mouth.

The baby thrust his thumb into his mouth
and lay content there with his half-closed eyes.
He had a sense of safeness in the warm
arms of his mother—quiet against her breast.
He turned his head toward her as her smile
caused him to pause and lift his wrinkled hands.

He waved his arms above him while his hands
tried helplessly to touch his mother's mouth.
He twisted at her robe until her smile
reassured him, and she loved him with her eyes.
She moved the quivering lips from aching breast—
the place where lips had been still glowing warm.

The mother felt her beating heart flood warm
as the baby clutched at her with seeking hands,
and she felt a filling warmth pervade her breast.
Smiling gently at the turned-down mouth,
she brushed the dampness from her eyes.
She looked at him again with gentle smile.

A finger pressing to his cheek brought out a smile
and stirred again the mother's heart to warm.
He gazed into her darkening eyes
as she reached down with soothing hands
to guide his faltering finger to his mouth.
He turned his head and burrowed for her breast.

Again, she held him warm against her breast.
Her fingers touched his mouth—she saw him smile.
Covering the infant's hands, she kissed the closing eyes.

# *Beauty*

Fragile loveliness…
Crystal waters
with a faint reflection
of the far-off, azure firmament.
Precious gems…
Clear diamonds, emeralds, topaz.
Shimmering waters
gently stirred by the humming breeze.
Transparent beauty…

Age and beauty…
Antiques.
Weatherbeaten cabin, long deserted
now falling to the ground.
Aged oak tree..
Knotted and gnarled by passing eras.
A face…
Altered by the years
from a thing of youthful color
to a wrinkled mask…
framed by hair as white as winter snow.
Ancient beauty…

Youth!
Lovelier than all else!
Hope! happiness! laughter!
All reflected in a smiling face...
Young eyes! red lips! round firm face!
Plans for the future...

These are beauty!

# The Closed Curtain

If I could part this dampened, mist-hid curtain,
walk through and then beyond the shrouded door,
I know I'd find you waiting in the shadows
and hold you close—try hard to keep you near.
The fading dream would slip back into blackness
where dreams are kept in deepest solitude
until they're summoned by a silent need
for one more glimpse of moments we once shared.
This curtain keeps us separate—apart—
the years together lost in fog of time,
but you are there beyond the shadows
while I must stand alone—earthbound for now.

# To Debbi

On the 5th of May 1957—
our anniversary fifteen—
a precious bundle came to us,
one blonde-haired infant girl
with eyes of grayish-green

to join her sister, who was eight
and her brother, age thirteen.

Now the years have passed—
her father and sister gone
and her nephew (born when she was eight),
but priceless memories remain
of those years before those loved ones
entered death's eternal gate.

Now this baby's birthday comes again—
and we must cling to all those years
and wipe away our tears.

# Child of Mary

On this day our Lord was born—
In a manger filled with hay,
Among the cows and horses,
In his humble bed he lay.

Outside the wind was blowing
And the snow was drifting down
And all was white and shining
In the little holy town.

Around small Jesus' head,
There shone an ethereal light,
Which awed the humble parents
Of the infant born that night.

Joseph and Mary watched their babe
As He lay in peaceful sleep,
And they vowed forever and ever
Their child with love to keep.

Through the cold, blustering night,
Three men trudged bravely on

To reach the place where Jesus lay
Ere that one bright star was gone.

At last they found the humble place
And knelt by the lowly bed,
And there, before the Christ-Child,
Each bowed his graying head.

While outside the wind blew strong
To pile the snow in drifts,
To the tiny new-born Savior,
They made their precious gifts.

# Resurrection

Death came and gently touched His brow
When Christ could bear the cross no more
And led Him to a silent tomb,
Where a great stone sealed the door.

"— And on the third day an angel came
And rolled the stone away—"
Out from the cold dark tomb He came
And into the golden day.

## *Daybreak*

There's a gray dawn creeping over the hill,
But the moon hangs on in the heavens still,
And the day must wait for the sun to rise,

Till the white stars fade and the moon gives way
To the glow of the morning sun's first ray,
And the night folds up and dies.

# Davi 1993

The grey metal shed
    stands with dented side.
The Raleigh bicycle sits
    in silence on its stand.
The wooden sled
    hangs listless on the wall.

Inside and down the hall,
    the door to your room
        is closed,
    holding our memories
        in quiet pain.

Sometimes we hear
    the ball hit the shed
    with a thud,
    the wheels of the bicycle
    on the drive,
    the sled's steel runners
    on the ice,

and the echoes of your presence
    fill the empty spaces
        in our hearts.

# In Memory of
# David M. Higgins, Jr.

And now we weep—
feel unutterable pain—
carry smothering guilt
that will remain.

What words so deep
were left unsaid?
What walls were built?
Why is he dead?

Now he lies in silent sleep —
the years stretch on and on.
The flowers bloom again — and wilt —
he's gone from us forever — gone —

# The Moon

The moon rose;
a pale yellow disc
It appeared,
then glided by.

The moon set;
A dim white phantom
It slipped
from the starlit sky.

## Deserted Derrick

Towering nigh above oil-stained lands,
A rotting wooden structure stands.
From the rude frame platform above
A great iron cable limply hangs,
Its lower end pulled loose from
The broken concrete base.
Halfway to the ground a splintered ladder

Sways. It makes a hollow clatter
When the wind comes in wild fury,
Darkened by the gritty sand,
Swirled from regions to the northwest—
And casts a veil of dust, obliterating space.
The slush-pit, once filled with black waste oil,
Is but a mass of heavy sinking tar;
And where the shanty tool-house once stood near,
Now lies a heap of blackened wood.
But over the forgotten tower there shines the
                              same bright star
That cast its rays upon the derrick in an
                              early year.

# *Drouth*

For weeks the sun has cast its scorching rays
to bake the earth and leave it cracked and sere—
the grass is brown and brittle with decay
and with each day more leafless limbs appear.
Famished birds scratch listlessly for worms
and scrabble on the ground for spindly seeds.
Beneath a fallen limb, a brown bug burrows
through the crumbling, dried-out weeds.
Dry leaves lie crumpled, crushed by lace-tied boots
or canvas shoes or by the barrow's wheel—
loose soil, drained and dull, conceals the roots
of gaunt gray scrub through which the black ants steal.

Grim ants and bugs and plants may feel their woes increase
if barren clouds drift by—with nothing to release.

# *Escape*

The sleek black cat slinks silent
through weeds wet from morning dew.
She stalks her prey with sly intent—
green eyes glint cold, malevolent.
Suddenly she springs limb high—
a streak wings out across the sky.

Two ruffled feathers grace the ground—
From treetop, notes of triumph sound.

# Death

The feathered form
struck the ground
with a thud—
beak and talons
charred black,
body limp
and still.

Overhead
the mimosa limb
brushed the singing wire.

# Early Morning in a Valley

Arrayed in robes of sparkling frost,
    the silent valley sleeps
        in wintry solitude.

A silver mist arises from a crystal stream
    and hovers in a pale cloud
        overhead.

Against a distant hillside,
    blue smoke curls from
        a blackened chimney-top
And lies suspended on the animated air.

    As a roseate glow steals over hoary fields,
    The sleeping valley wakes to greet the rising sun.

# To My Chicks on a Rainy Day

Yesterday when the sun was warm,
You were all so lively and gay—
So eager to tug at the yielding grass
And run about in your heedless way.

Yet today you droop dejectedly
And stare at the world in bedraggled dismay—
Could it be you delighted in yesterday's sun
And are sorry it rained today?

## Ebon on Snow

I stand here looking out at all the snow
on branches drooping from their heavy load.
Red-winged blackbirds sit hunched and still
until one jerks its wings in startled flight—
then all the blackbirds flutter limb to limb
knocking snow lumps to the icy ground.

One dark bird drops quickly to the ground
to look for bits of seed beneath the snow.
I hear the creaking crack of laden limb
as branches give up grudgingly their load—
suddenly all birds take off in frightened flight
and, settling on a nearby bush, sit quiet and still.

The blackbirds, gathering, grouping, waiting still,
espy some bits of plunder on the frozen ground.
They grab the loot and take to upward flight
and hurry back to laden limbs of snow.
One bird picks up an extra crumb to add to load
he's taking to his mate stranded on a limb.

The mate makes up her mind to leave the limb,
so, tired of staying silent there and still,
she flies down to look for food to load
and bring back from the frigid ground.
The crumbs she finds are colored like the snow
and one she grabs and wings in triumphal flight.

Two crows that join the other birds in flight
alight on one snow-covered quivering limb
that bends low from the heaps of drifting snow
and clings tenaciously to trunk of tree so still.
The black cloud swarms toward the whitened ground
searching for more shreds of scraps to load.

The black horde shakes the shifting load
of snow from branches, then takes flight
to seek out more affluent ground.
Where snow, dropped softly from a shaken limb,
lies in piles of white to glisten still,
the heaps are hidden by another cloud of falling snow.

Red-streaked wings take flight and loose the load
from weakened limb that brushes ground
still sleeping underneath the covering snow.

# *Emblem*

The banner we were taught to give esteem
is draped across the backs of those who dare
to give no homage to their own. They deem
that token as just something else to wear—
not honored emblem to imbue the crowd
with patriotism and a high regard—
a thing of which we all can well be proud.
They think of it as something to discard.
The flag at one time typified respect—
we watched it pass with patriotic pride,
but now when it is shown, we can expect
a few to view it only to deride.

Still, some who see the flag will stand
and greet with dignity the symbol of our land.

## *Firefly*

Bright flicks of light
as dusk sets in
and darkness begins—
suddenly a golden glow
seems to come and go
while a few feet away
a flickering spark
lights up the dark.

# Four Years Old

Her long white dress
catching on
the rough bark,
the child clutched
the towering tree.
Fingers and toes
cramped tight,
she made her way
slowly up the round
trunk
until she reached
the first low branches
then pulled higher
toward the top.
"Come down!"
her brother called,
"You're much too high."
Hanging on
to an outflung
limb,
the child
tight-closed

her lips—
then,
looking down,
sang out—
"I'm not
on the tip-top
leaf!"

# Helda, the Stripdown

had
a Model-T frame
four wheels, wooden-spoked—
a coat of all colors,
sand and sun-soaked.
Sometimes
Helda balked—
had to be coaxed
with oil and gasoline,

spark plugs and wires—
and Helda would answer
with loud backfires.
The guys who owned her
we often had doubt of,
because—well,
Helda was
Helda get into
and Helda get out of.

# Highway

The soft cloud
curls
like a miniature
tornado
blending into
the blue
background
of a
Tennessee sky.
The green trees
hem the highway
from the onslaught
of traffic.
Around the bend
a bridge
thrusts its way,
above the hysterics
of the fast lanes.

At the top
of
the hill
cars and clouds
collide.

# Gatsby (nicknamed Goofy)

The naked baby bluejay lay limp
across the rock where he had fallen—
his weak neck badly twisted in the plunge—
but he was still alive, for I could see
his tiny chest rise up and down. We fed
him hourly with milk and egg yolks
laced with wheat germ meal. He learned

to love the mixed-up brew. For days
he ate with bald head upside down; then
gradually he feathered out and bloomed.
Goofy liked the backyard when we took him out
to get his daily exercise—he perched upon
a fallen limb we found for him. He'd hang
on tight with clutching claws, and through
the green grass skitter to our feet and hop
up on our shoes and stand upright. With
pride, he peered back at the wilderness of lawn.
He took short rides with us around the countryside—
once shared our picnic lunch at Withrow Springs.
Now Goofy is a seasoned traveler—he's been
four times with us to Bloomington.

# King Edward

In England nineteen-thirty-six,
King Edward was in quite a fix.
He wanted his throne and his lady, too,
But the Cabinet said that wouldn't do.
So he lingered along for quite awhile
Trying to get them both by wile.
He finally decided to give it up,
And with fair Wally forever to sup.
Then for other lands he did embark,
And left fair England to the Duke of York.

## *Interlude*

My body falling,
my mind etching
the words
"This is it!"
I've waited too long.
I paid lip service
to God, but
my heart was
not wholly in it.
My hurt and hate
when Davi left
us, or did God
take him? I
wasn't ever sure.
Now I have
another chance—
to ponder
all the ins
and outs of life—
to thank God
for all He's
given—after all

he gave us
Davi for twenty
years—a lifetime—
his—Davi's.
I feel that
Davi is in
God's hands
and God,
the Creator,
holds the
secret of what
is best for us.

 So now I
hope and pray
that I will
never, while
I have life,
forget that
God is
the beginning,
the end,

and our
hope and
promise.

## Life

Three-score years
plus ten and four
I've lived upon
this earth.
I've tasted much
of joy and sorrow,
love and hatred,
death and birth.

I've seen the robin
and the bluejay,
the cardinal
and the dove
match the earth's
varied colors
and, yes,
the sky above.

I've seen
the hand of God
in the sun's
piercing beam—

the clearness
of raindrops—
the shadowed snow
beside a stream.

I've heard
the unreal rhythm
of the wailing
wind's refrain.
I've seen the sun
through parting clouds
after hours
of chilling rain.

I've seen
the magic sparkle
in the brown eyes
of a child
recounting an adventure
with a smile.
 I've heard
the quick shy laughter

as a small girl
caught a ball—
I've seen her face
light up in wonder
when she heard her
mother's call.

I've seen the look
of innocence
on a newborn's
wrinkled face,
and the smile
of happy triumph
from a boy
who's won a race.

And I've seen
the silent
touch of death
that took
that boy's
last breath.

So much of living
saddens
giving pain—
the memories
of sunshine
helps to ease
the lonely rain.

# Last Resort

One lone fly
buzzing around the room
flashes past the glow
of the table lamp—
skims across
the rows of books—
lights a second—
seems to sense
the swatter's presence.
The morning papers
lie neglected
while the flitting fly
holds court.
Swat!
Quiet reigns.
Reading ritual resumed.

## La Vista

I think back on the years of the depression
with mist-filled eyes—
I see the deprivation as a force
to build upon. My shoes were lined inside
with pasteboard cut from cereal cartons
or backs of writing tablets
(Big Chief for a nickel)
used for school. These soles served well
until my foot came down upon a gravel,
and pain refused the soles.
I wore dresses made from flour sacks—
checks and stripes and flowery prints,
and, sometimes, looking down, I could see
"made from wheat" printed on my knee.
Meals came from our backyard garden—
turnip greens, Kentucky Wonders,
tomatoes (red and ripe)
and small thin-skinned potatoes
(boiled until the skin would slip.)
A way behind the house, the hogpen
held our ham, salt pork and bacon—
and we always kept a cow for milk

and sometimes nanny goats
(their milk was rank)!
We had to stake the cow where grass grew
in the ditches near the street. She had
to be short-tethered. With her long curving horns
she would duck her head and try to hook
a passerby. On Sundays we had eggs
for breakfast (I would find them in the nest).
After church we had crisp chicken
cooked in lard in a black iron frying pan.
I pulled weeds for spending money,
peddled papers once a week
and threw Piggly Wiggly food ads
house to house.
But weekends were for having fun.
I pedaled around on my second-hand bike,
picked up small stones to hit with sticks,
and (using my last dime if I had one)
on Saturday afternoons I watched Tom Mix
as he rode the range
at La Vista, the local movie house.

## Lost

Sometimes he walks in the rain—
lets the drops run down his back
in futile attempt to still the pain

that he feels at the hopeless lack
of her presence in his life.
Often times he loses track

of the hours and hours of strife
in trying to deal with his loss—
like the cutting edge of a knife.

Through the endless night he'll toss
and turn—and seek relief as he sleeps,
but this is his own heavy cross

to bear, And he keeps
her close as he walks in the rain—
as he walks in the rain and weeps.

# The Bindweed

They call it
the bindweed.
It curls and coils
all around.
It covers
the fence posts,
wrapping and trapping
until no fence
can be found.
It reaches out
tendrils
to smother the maple
till the dead empty limbs
are sheathed in green leaves,
darkly bright.

All over the fences—
all over the branches—
the pink and white bugles
hold sway.

The poor lowly bindweed
is magically blooming—
      Morning glory
           welcomes the day.

# Mary, Age 2

A laughing dynamo, she speeds across
    the toy-strewn floor
in sometimes losing race,
to catch a fleeting glimpse
of the rumbling city bus.

She stands and holds with tiny hands
    the grilled and guarded door,
smile wide upon her face.
Once winning in her wild attempts,
she looks and then runs back to us.

## My Pet Hate

Never again when I'm lying in bed
Do I want a cat sleeping at my head:
For when I'm drowsy, I loathe to hear
A kitten purring close to my ear.

# Mother

The sweetest and kindest of them all
Is a loving mother's gentle call.
As her hair grows from dark to gray,
She strives to help us more each day.
A loving hand is put on your warm head
Showing your mother stands over your bed.
If asked, you say, "Sure, I love my mother."
But could you love as well any other?
Her eyes of deepest brown or clearest blue
Gaze at you with a love that is true.
So love your mother with a clear mind.
And show your love by being kind.

# Mother's Death

In dark of winter
Death captures faces
ashen from old age—
his life, her life
form a catalyst
from bits of paper
cast away.

Young man creeps barefoot
across the cold floor,
never thinking.
Down a cobbled lane,
he walks into the rainstorm
seeking passages to survival.

He can't go home—
the ones that he remembers
as a child are gone.
In his mind, shots ring out—
memories press down—
he sees the woman fall
in the room of the old farmhouse.

His parents—
after forty years together,
one is gone—
the other sits grappling with the past.

The young man sits at a table
eating cheese—crumbling crackers
cover the words he writes.

Leaving his new world behind,
he begins to write about
what he can't forget.

He hears the pines whispering—
remembers eyes staring.
He remembers the beginning of love,
misfortune, music—looks up a passage
from the First Book of Timothy, 6:7.
(For we brought nothing
into this world, and it is certain
we can carry nothing out.)

The moving light brings back
visions of a young girl,
music, and trees.
The wind blowing clouds
brings it all back—
dark hidden rocks, red-flowering fields,
joyful voices, sifting snow,
months in Montana.

Memory keeps slipping down hill
freezing into frames—
death, the falling woman.
One by one, the thoughts surface
and melt into nothing.

Winter withers the spirit.

# Of JLM, Three-Year-Old

"My son's a rowdy fellow—
Tough, arrogant, all boy."
Dad was quite enthusiastic
About his heir, his pride and joy.
Till the mother interrupted
And gave the boasting dad a start
When very calmly she announced,
"Your son wants a doll and a cart."

## And Now We Know

Walking out in the cold still morning
to get the early paper, I looked
to the east and the rose-hued dawn.
The cooing call of a dove to its mate
fell on my ears like a benediction,
and I raised my eyes to see the bird
etched against the bare tree limbs
in the lightening sky.

Coming back in, I heard the far-off wail
of a siren. The beauty of the sky faded
as I recalled the devastating scenes
from last night's TV—the curls of smoke,
the broken glass, and the soot-blackened
faces of the injured people being carried
from the world trade center.

# Moving the Sheep

Curly cream-colored sheep
pushing one against the other
block the road
while the herder sits
astride his saddle—
silent, unmoving as
smoke coils up
from his dangling
thin-wrapped cigarette.

His roan stallion raises
one nervous hoof
and paws the dust-filled air.

Edging forward slowly,
bumper barely touching
bleating ewes,
the battered pickup
pushes a path
through the herd
that slowly opens up ahead.

Reflected in the mirror,
the shambling sheep
close in behind the truck
and reclaim the road.

# Old Man at Bedtime

He slumps, head nodding,
in his blue night shirt.
Half-closed eyes see
disillusions
in the feeble flames
fading into darkness.
From the worn
wooden chair
the gray cat eyes
the scattered crumbs
on the blue stone plate.
As the low-turned lamp
reflects the embers' glow,
the radio emits
an unintelligible hum—
and the dull night drags on.

# My Uncle's Death

He was walking
slowly
on the shoulder
of the road
when the car
struck him down.

It dragged him
underneath
even though
he grabbed
the bumper

grasping it

until
his fingers
loosed their grip
and the car went on its way.

When they picked my uncle up,
his fingers were still.

# One Day in October

I kneel on the damp grass
and place the three red
rose-buds by the image
on the stone—gray eyes
stare back into my own that
look beyond the slope to
the pond below where ducks
swim and geese leave trails
of gray-white feathers
in the grass.
By the reeds on the bank,
a boy in faded jeans sits
dreaming—and my dreams
fade to memory—the boy
that was is here beneath
the stone and by the pond—
forever here
the boy,
the pond,
the stone.

## No Return

Behind a flat hot parking lot
the building stands—no trees
to break the monotony—
in the lot itself
a faded blue Honda and a gray Mercedes
side by side.
Near the street
a few marigolds
in scraggly splendor.
I walk through the open door
into a dreary lobby
where an old lady sits
short strings of hair
dangling in her eyes.
Staring vacantly
she slowly pulls
at a broken fingernail
until the blood flows.
Nearby a frail man
with thin salt-and-pepper beard
drums his fingers
against the arms

of a cane-backed wheelchair.
His left leg hangs limp
the right swings back and forth.
On a small platform
three girl singers
from the local high school
wait to entertain
the old folks
as a red-haired boy
strikes a note
on the ancient player-piano.
Walking down the long
Congoleum-covered corridor,
I catch a glimpse
of a cushion
picturing Niagara Falls
a snapshot of a smiling man
sporting a flat straw hat
an open Bible
lying on a bed.
Feeling the curious watching eyes

I recall a path
through a snow-locked woods
and a small gray rabbit
caught in a steel trap.

# O.P.O. at the Vet's

Through the grilled door
on your carrier
you look past me—
ignoring me
because you're here
behind bars
unable to walk around
and sniff at doors
to try to figure out
what's behind them
or to try to find
a way out of this place—
here comes a person
with a hose
and a bottle of liquid—
you know what that means
and look at me as if
to say, "Not again!"
You look as if you wish
you were back
at the Old Post Office
where you were found.

# Poverty

Gravely you sit in your rickety high chair.
Already poverty has left its mark
upon your baby features. Your great dark eyes
are fixed in an unwavering stare
on the empty bowl before you.

In your tiny baby hands you clutch
a small and battered pewter cup
which, instinctively, you have lifted up
against your swollen gum to touch
and help your teeth break through.

Although your life has only just begun,
too soon you have started the bout
with poverty. You have learned to do without
the things you need. You're such a little one
to be so wan and cold and blue.

# Refinery

Where not so long ago the great wheels
 swiftly turned,
And men, begrimed with oil and dirt and sweat,
Toiled to keep each engine running,
Now sprawls a maze of ghostly buildings,
Long since reduced to ruin by the
Raging fire which once swept through them.
They stand—a grim reminder of the days
When the little town was booming.
No longer do their walls resound
With the dull roar of pounding engines—
Only scuttling rats break the monotonous,
 melancholy quiet.

# Quiet Hummer

On a leaf-clad limb of the redbud,
a hummingbird sits—scanning its space
in silence—diminutive wings folded.
Suddenly a flash of blurred wings
streaks through the air
straight to the sycamore—
then sits in silence once again.

# Power of the Pecos

Between its dull alkaline banks
The sullen stream moves slowly on
Like some lazy serpent writhing over
An expanse of dry and barren sod,
Not caring that above it reigns
An unclouded azure firmament.

The muddy waters creep along,
Ever slow, unchangeable and grim,
Only a sunken gully extending its way
Through a land of fruitless soil—
The only vegetation the brittle salt cedar
That lines its soggy banks.

And yet—the land through which the
Pecos winds its stolid length
Is a land which holds within its bosom
Endless riches. Beneath that sandy soil
Lies a power that stretches over all the world
to reign like some black king of darkest Africa.

The Pecos River is a proud river,
For it is a part of that barren land
Which furnishes the world that ever-powerful ruler—
    Oil.

# The Dry Devil's River

A dry and rock-strewn gully made its way
in aimless fashion through the park in our
small southwest Texas town. The park
through which it wandered was my playground—
with mesquites and oaks to climb like Tarzan
and with stones to border rooms and
close in cooking fire. I'd bake potatoes
in the red-hot coals until they charred
and blackened on the outside—dead-white,
half-cooked, half-raw inside the peels.
A swinging bridge hung near the roadway
where a concrete overflow was used for cars.
This was the Devil's River, dry and dead—
until one day the clouds kept piling up
and turning dark and darker—thunder roared.
Lightning broke the sky in two. The clouds
dropped sheets of rain, and in the distance
could be heard the sound of water coming
down the dry stream bed. The water made
a moving wall, uprooting trees that scraped
the banks and caught on jutting rocks. It
spread across the road and reached our house—

then flowed across the porch and to the door.
Our old Whippet took us out—it spun its wheels.
The motor stopped, then caught—we slowly
reached high ground. Days later we came back
to view the damage from the flood.
Our house still there—
but filled with mud and silt—
half-hidden by the broken limbs
from massacred mesquite trees.

Above the slime and mire of the riverbed,
one end of the dangling foot-bridge
hung from the slippery, soggy banks
of the dry Devil's River.

# Saturday Night

The blare of taxis
As they roar about the streets,
Cutting corners—traveling madly—
Carrying people who are
Going places—
On Saturday Night.

Store-windows decorated—
Some with costly jewels and dresses,
Some with clothing cheap and gaudy,
Others advertising bargains—
For Saturday Night.

The general confusing hubbub
Of the people on the streets—
Some aimless, wandering around the square,
Others window shopping;
And all downtown just because—
It's Saturday Night.

## Soft Wind

The soft wind stirs the lake's unruffled calm.
It gently blows through thicket's shrubs and trees
and brings about an aromatic sensual balm
that soothes the heart and sets the mind at ease.
With magic lilting touch, that same light breeze
frets the small wild roses by the fence.
conveys the buzzing of the yellow bees,
and teases with the spring's elusive scents.
A cardinal views the soft wind with suspense,
and from the slender limb that slightly sways,
unfolds with hesitance his scarlet wings.
He flies straight to his nesting mate and thence
he perches near. He voices his celestial praise,
tones down his song and gently, softly, sings.

# See-Saw

A see-saw, merry-go-round
built by an older brother—
I sat on one end;
he sat on the other.

One long board fixed on a post
with seats from a grocery crate,
fastened down with rusted nails,
made strong to hold our weight.

The board worked fine—
went round and round
till my brother jumped off
and I went down.

My right leg caught
beneath the board.
The nail thrust through—
my calf felt gored.

Impaling my leg
on the rusted nail

left an ugly scar
to end my tale.

# Spring Sonnet

The rain streams down upon the new-flowered trees,
washing clean the feeders waiting for the birds.
It trickles through the grass in endless search
for some low-sunken stretch to catch its flow.
The pink of redbuds stains the drenched ground,
mixing crumpled petals with the golden glow
of dandelions and yellow daffodils.
Magnolias open blooms from tight-closed fists
spreading ghostly clouds against the dark
and glossy thickly-clustered leaves
and shadowing the violet's bashful face.

One lonely limb hangs down in disarray—
a victim of the spring's last crippling snow.

## Six O'Clock, Boomtown

The gritty Chevy truck
squeals to a stop.
Roustabouts—
grimy clothes oil-soaked,
sweat creasing sun-charred faces,
leap to the ground.
Tinny sounds from
Red's Cafe—
Honky-Tonk Blues playing
on the battered nickelodeon.
Boisterous voices hail
the black-eyed waitress
as she swipes a dingy rag
across the counter.

The dirt-streaked men
plop down
on the twirling stools.

# Summer Storm

Sullen clouds hang low
    upon the hills
pressing the sultry air
    down into the valley.
Suddenly jagged lightning
    flashes and
rumbling clouds pelt rain
    onto the thirsty fields.

# The Boy and the Fish

He sits there quietly somber by the stream,
his cane pole dangling near a sunken log.
Dark eyes hold shadows of a drifting dream
disrupted by the flop of slick-skinned frog,
his legs are outstretched on the pitted rock;
his fingers gently hold the rustic pole,
the slight tan hand at times inclined to mock
the perch that pulls the line across the hole.
Still he sits and plays the fish and string
till, suddenly, the angling line grows taut.
He raises pole and starts the circling swing
to bring his catch aground. The fish is caught!

Then gently loosening the jagged hook,
he gives his trembling fish back to the brook.

# The Balloons

One rain-dripped morning
I pushed open
my back screen
and, looking up,
saw seven helium balloons
caught high in the mimosa tree.

They floated in from somewhere.
Pink, yellow, blue—
they all swayed
to the touch of the wind.
They shimmered
with the taste of the rain.
They floated in from somewhere—
I don't know where—
a celebration on the square,
the opening of a new mall,
or maybe
a roadside mailbox
marking a child's birthday
celebration.

They floated in on a gentle wind
from somewhere.

I climbed the tree
and grasped the tangled strings
of three balloons—
one blue, one pink, one yellow.
    I held on tightly
        to the pink and yellow.

The third balloon
the blue one—
    I let it go
        and watched it rise
            and float away
                until it disappeared.

## Bears

Bears are for loving
        and hitting and hugging—
for sitting on dressers and shelves.

For making a child
        feel sheltered—secure.

Bears come in all sizes,
        shapes and disguises—
scraps of gingham and calico too.
They come in all colors—
        in yellow and purple and blue.

You say they're not real?

To the child who owns them,
        the bears are alive
and as real as their friends
        that they play with—
as real as the children themselves.

Bears are for loving
and hitting and hugging—
for sitting on dressers and shelves.

# Touching

If I could meet you when the day begins,
slow-walking in the dim that speaks of dawn,
perhaps we could find autumn coming on
with changing leaves and almost cooling winds
that blow against the face. We might could meet
when sun is riding high across the sky
above the vagrant clouds meandering by—
one day like this would be a day complete.
We possibly could meet as day begins to end—
the two of us discovering that path
that slowly winds to aftermath
when streaks of vibrant colors mix and blend.

And I'll be waiting—trembling but serene
to meet you once again beyond death's screen.

# Twilight

Long shadows soften and disappear
As the last glow of sunset fades
In the west. A tranquil hush
Settles over the darkened countryside
And hovers there momentarily,
Until the still quiet is broken
By the low hum of the crickets—
And the dusk merges into night.

# The Dive

The old TP Tavern was a honky-tonk,
just beyond the city limits of McCamey
    on Highway Sixty-seven—
    east of town.

Plain and spread out, with a dance floor
sanded down and shining, big enough
    for every one to come
    and listen to the sound

of all the smaller dance bands
and some more famous too—big name bands,
    whose groups of players
    sometimes came around.

Through the week it looked deserted,
with its tumbleweeds and sand,
    but early on each weekend,
    the honky-tonk was found

to be a spot for fun and jiving
and gathering with friends.
    TP Tavern was a Mecca
        for that small West Texas town.

## U.S. Eighty West

I drive the lonesome
U.S. Eighty West
staring ahead
at sunbaked blacktop
outstretched along
the barren miles.
The Goodyear tires
make a steady drone.
A scissortail sits singing
on the barbed wire fence
where longhorn cattle stand
and rub their necks
on rusting barricade
and flick their tails
at stinging gnats
and biting flies.
Tumbleweeds clean sweep
a path ahead as I
watch the colors
streak the sky,
the sun fade into
the cooling dusk,

and the long highway
stretches into the night.

# Walking on Hot Coals

Biggest brother was given
the chore of baby-sister
watching—but something
caught his interest
and his eyes were
somewhere else
and his mind
was in the distance
when I, a toddling babe,
walked upon hot coals.
The gray ash
covering the embers
called my curious feet
as a magnet draws a nail—
the screams and blisters
rose and broke
loosing the rain
from my eyes
and I crawled
and cried again
as I had
before I learned

to stand upright
and walk.

# Why

The white tissue tears
as she wraps the sweater
carefully and places it
in the white box.

A wistful smile appears
as she scans the crumpled
letter and gently faces it
downward in the white box.

Dreams, illusions, fears
chain to form a fetter
and lock the empty spaces
in the white box.

# Wet Fields

At dawn on a rain-swept hillside,
With a soft breeze ruffling my hair,
I stand gazing down at the valley,
View it and find it fair.

The rich loam newly broken
Lies black and wet from the rain,
And I stand in reverent wonder
Seeing spring reborn again.

# Woodland Trail

I wish that I could share this day
with you—
and the winding path
I follow
down the grass-strewn slope.

The shady trail
Where dancing rays of light break through—
The heavy foliage
of towering trees—
A robin calling to his listening mate—
I hear
and
think of you.

# What is Age?

I'm old at seventy, you say?
That's really quite unfair!
You're judging by encroaching gray
that's uncoloring my hair—
the slower walk and cautious air,
the hands that grip the rail
when stepping down the stair,
the eyes that sometimes fail.
I mow the grass and weed the beds
of tulips, daffodils and pinks;
I prune the shrubbery to shreds
and clean both kitchen sinks.
At seventy I take long walks,
rake endless bags of leaves.
I listen to environment talks.
I ride my bike with ease.

I feel that I am aging well,
but only time the truth will tell.

## Fall

Gold leaves, brown leaves,
Heaped up by the winds—
And every changing, drifting leaf
An autumn message sends.

'Tis fall! The woods are calling!
Nuts are on the ground and,
Sheltered by the falling leaves,
Are waiting to be found.

# All Hallow's Eve

I sit here wondering—have I enough
Mr. Goodbars, Hershey's kisses, Tootsie Roll's
to satisfy the ghosts to come? The doorbell
rings—outside the door stand several spooky
youngsters holding bags, expecting treats.
I toss in candy bars in gold-foil wrappers.
The orange bags are stuffed with all the loot
that's showered upon these costumed kids.
The children leave and I turn back to watch TV.
The newsman gives his spiel, the football players
prance across the screen in padded suits
laughing over winning their last game.

The pictures change—Mozambique, Somaliland—
in front of me are starving children.
Their ribs stand out against their yellow skin,
stomachs distended, cheekbones prominent
under dark staring eyes. Cracked lips—
no treats for them—just silent, grim despair.

That evening
at the table

I cramped my toes
around the chair rung,
pushed my plate aside—
and cried.

# *Yesterday*

We left him standing
in the kitchen—
yesterday—
said, "We'll be back soon,"
but he was gone
when we returned.

The shrilling of the phone
shook us from our beds—
3:51 a.m.—
this gray waiting room,
the receptionist talking
to an idle nurse—
the faint wail of a siren—

From down the hall
a door opened—
the doctor walked slowly
toward us—
wiping his hands.

# *Your Father*

You do not know him very well
For he usually works all day,
And though he's always home at night,
That's your time to be away.

You seldom try to know him—
To learn what's in his heart,
And if he tries to talk with you,
You seldom do your part.

Someday you'll wish you'd understood
How he was hurt by your neglect,
And that through the years he merely tried
To gain your love and respect.

# Hats Off to Dorothy Lindquist

This lady
(at four score years plus six)
makes me feel ashamed—
I say that I'm too old
(at three score ten and four)
to work so hard
just trying to keep up
my house and yard—
yet she has needed works
for which she's aimed
and taken on
and carried out.
Working to help others
in their bout with poverty,
she makes her years an asset—
keeps going on these trips
to other lands
to help the people
there beset
with lacks
which we cannot conceive.
She goes and helps them

to believe
that there are somewhere
on this earth
people who value
every person's worth.
This lady is an inspiration
to those my age and younger
to bestir themselves
to helping those who hunger
and try to bring
to those in need
(in our own nation)
love and succor.
To this great lady—
Dorothy Lindquist—
HATS OFF—
we salute you.

# One Day

I watched two rabbits
in my backyard—
one hopped away—
the other followed.
I hoped they would stay
among the flowers
in the hollowed spaces—
little rabbit faces
gamboling there between
the blooms and clover.
Sometimes
one looks around
as if to say,
"The game is over."
I hope they come again

       Today.

*The End*

**Mary Elizabeth Brantley Harvey** was born in east Texas on October 8, 1920. She wrote her first poetry while in high school in the oil fields of Texas. As a senior, she composed the class poem; however, a classmate read it as she was too timid.

Later she moved to Arkansas where she contributed to the "Ozark Moon" column edited by Walter Lemke of the University of Arkansas' Department of Journalism.
She submitted poems to various journals during her days in Fayetteville.

After her marriage to Charles S. Harvey, who became an officer in the U.S. Army, she spent time in Oklahoma, Michigan, Minnesota, North Carolina, Texas, and in Germany. At retirement, Charles and Mary bought a house in Fayetteville, Arkansas, and returned there to begin a more relaxed civilian life; Charles did not live to enjoy his golden years with his beloved wife.

After that great loss, Mary pulled herself together, began to write again and returned to the University to further her education. Though a little less robust, she still maintains her residence in Fayetteville and continues to write and publish poetry.